MORE

LOVE

Experiencing God's Love

D0711001

MORE
LOVE

Experiencing God's Love

Betsy Duffey

ISBN-13: 979-8646876639

Dear God,

Bless the reader of this book
to know Your love.

May each word be a blessing
that opens hearts and minds to You.
May each experience bring an
awakening to the love
that is all around us.

Let each one who holds this book
find the deep love You have for them.

Thank you, Lord,
for the love You will show
through these words.

Amen

CONTENTS

1
Be Still

In the middle of your busy life,
God waits.
Love waits.

Be still.

Sit for a moment in your favorite chair.
Stop and stand in a spot of sunlight.
Shut the door to your office.
Pull over by the side of the road.
Close your eyes in the waiting room.
Don't wake the children yet.

Breathe deeply.
Ask God to come into that stillness.
Ask love to come.

Be still and find love.

Let God have you,
and let God love you
and don't be surprised if your heart
begins to hear music you've
never heard and your feet learn
to dance as never before.
Max Lucado

Be still and know that I am God.
Psalm 46:10

2
Beautiful Thoughts

Think.

Think of the vastness of the ocean
looking out from the shore.
Of moss covered rocks
along a garden path.
Of the night sky dotted
with a million stars.
Of clouds billowing
in the blue sky.

Every memory resides in
your incredible brain.

When you think of beautiful things,
each thought is a gift
from our beautiful God.
He loves you that much.

How precious to me are
your thoughts, O God!
How vast is the sum of them!
Were I to count them,
they would outnumber
the grains of sand.
When I awake,
I am still with you.
Psalm 139:17-18

The most significant gifts are the ones
most easily overlooked. Small, everyday
blessings: woods, health, music,
laughter, memories, books, family,
friends, second chances, warm
fireplaces, and all the footprints scattered
throughout our days.
Sue Monk Kidd

3
Baby Love

You are holding a small baby
on your shoulder. His tiny body is
wrapped in a soft cotton blanket.
His warm weight presses against you.

Your hand rests on his back.
You feel love for him.
No expectations. No conditions.
You rock back and forth to soothe
him as he sleeps.

Close your eyes and imagine God
holding you this way.
Firm. Warm.
Rocking you gently.
Feeling love for you.
No expectations. No conditions.
This is His love for you.

My heart is not proud, O Lord,
my eyes are not haughty;
I do not concern myself with great
matters or things too wonderful for me.
But I have stilled and quieted my soul;
like a weaned child with its mother,
like a weaned child is my soul within me.
Psalm 131:1-2

We love God
because he first loved us.
We long for God
because he first longed for us.
We reach for God
because he first reached for us.
Ruth Haley Barton

4
Receive Love

Sit quietly.
Breathe deeply.
Close your eyes.
Rest your hands on your knees,
palms up.

Imagine God's love pouring down
into your open hands.
His love fills your hands to overflowing.
The abundance of His love for you spills
out around you.

Now, press your full hands to your heart.
Receive His love for you.

Repeat often throughout the day.
His love is always available to you.
Just receive it.

If you have never known
the power of God's love,
then maybe it is because
you have never asked to know it –
I mean really asked,
expecting an answer.
Frederick Buechner

How great is the love
the Father has lavished on us,
that we should be called
children of God!
And that is what we are!
1 John 3:1

5
Hold My Hand

Sit quietly with your eyes closed
and hold one hand in the other.

Feel the strength of your hands.
Soft skin.
Hard knuckles.
Firm muscles.

With eyes still closed, imagine that it is
God holding your right hand.
Your left hand becomes His hand.
How does it feel to be held?

Throughout your day stop
and hold your hand.
God is with you.
He holds that hand.
He loves you.

For I am the Lord your God,
who takes hold of your right hand
and says to you, Do not fear;
I will help you.
Isaiah 41:13

To be known and not loved is our
greatest fear. But to be fully known and
truly loved is, well, a lot like
being loved by God.
Timothy Keller

6
Who You Are

Jesus says you are:

A child of God.
Chosen.
Light.
Valuable.
Salt.
Created by God.
Capable.
Worthy.
Dearly loved.
His friend.

Today, remember who Jesus
says that you are.
Choose one name.
Write it down and carry it with you.
He loves you.

Surely goodness and love
will follow me all the days of my life,
and I will dwell in the house of
the Lord forever.
Psalm 23:6

To fall in love with God
is the greatest romance;
to seek him the greatest adventure;
to find him the greatest
human achievement.
Saint Augustine

7
Delight and Joy

Something about animals
delights and amuses us.

Consider:
A cat lolling in a sunbeam.
A pile of sleeping puppies.
The round, spiky hedgehog.
Zany, playful baby goats.
A whale breaking the water surface.

All creatures great and small give us
beauty, delight and joy.
Our good God made the animals.
How much He loves us!

With each creature
He shows His love to you.
Notice animals today. Feel His love.

But ask the animals,
and they will teach you,
or the birds of the air,
and they will tell you;
or speak to the earth,
and it will teach you,
or let the fish of the sea
inform you.
Job 12:7-8

Every time you feel in God's creatures
something pleasing and attractive,
do not let your attention be arrested by
them alone but, passing them by,
transfer your thought to God and say,
"Oh, my God, if Thy creatures are so full
of beauty, delight, and joy, how infinitely
more full of beauty, delight, and joy art
Thou, Thyself, Creator of all!"
Nicodemus of the Holy Mountain

14

8
Blossoming

Your heart is a rose bud,
shut tight against the dangers
of the world. Close your eyes
and sit with this image.
Your beauty and fragrance
are closed and guarded.

Feel the warm light of God's love
surrounding you –
beckoning you to open.
Slowly begin, one petal at a time.
Open to the sunlight until the
rose petals of your
heart are fully open to God's light.

In His love you are safe.
You are delightful.
Beautiful. Fragrant. Loved.

All beautiful you are, my darling;
there is no flaw in you.
Song of Songs 4:7

Now, with God's help,
I shall become myself.
Soren Kierkegard

9
Talk to Jesus

Sit down with a cup of coffee or tea.
Make time for a visit with Jesus
just like you would with a good friend.

Imagine Him sitting,
unhurried, across from you.

Have a talk with Him.

Tell Him:
What you are thinking.
What makes you smile.
What hurts you.
How He can help you.

You are valuable and loved.
Sit with your friend, Jesus.
He loves this time with you.

Come near to God
and he will come near to you.
James 4:8

Lift up your heart to Him during
your meals and in company;
the least little remembrance will
always be the most pleasing to Him.
One need not cry out very loudly;
He is nearer to us than we think.
Brother Lawrence

10
Love Me

Think of a favorite name of Jesus.
Shepherd.
Bridegroom.
Teacher.
Deliverer.

Breathe in your name of Jesus.
Breathe out the words:
Love me.

Shepherd...Love me.
Bridegroom...Love me.
Teacher...Love me.
Deliverer...Love me.
Jesus...Love me.

Breathe this prayer often today.
It is a prayer that Jesus will answer.

Call to me and I will answer you
and tell you great and unsearchable
things you do not know.
Jeremiah 33:3

Looking back, I find it remarkable how
easily I accepted ideas about God as
substitutes for direct experience of him.
It took me a long time to begin
to know God through my heart
and not simply my head.
David Benner

11
Lost and Found

You may feel lost.
But you are not lost.
You are in a room.
It is part of a house or building.
It is part of a city.
Which is part of a state.
And country. And planet.
And solar system.

In the bigness of the world
you might feel small.
But God knows where you are.
He created the universe and He knows
right where you are in it.
He cares for you.
You might feel lost.
But you are seen by God.
Feel His presence with you today.

If I go up to the heavens, you are there;
if I make my bed in the depths,
you are there.
If I rise on the wings of the dawn,
if I settle on the far side of the sea,
even there your hand will guide me,
your right hand will hold me fast.
Psalm 139:8-10

Long ago I came to the
total assurance
that God loves me,
God knows where I am
every second of the day,
and God is bigger than
any problem life's circumstances
can throw at me.
Charles Stanley

12
Sunrise

Think of God's love.
His love is like the sun,
rising up every morning
bringing warmth and light.
Nothing can stop it.

Think of that light coming to you.
Cresting the horizon.
Moving across boundaries.
Over walls.
Through windows.
Into the cracks of your heart.

Stay still and let the light come.
It cannot be stopped by anyone.
It cannot be stopped by anything.
Like the sun rises, so His love rises,
filling you with warmth and light.

Love is larger than the
walls which shut it in.
Corrie Ten Boom

Then Jesus told them this parable:
Suppose one of you has a hundred
sheep and loses one of them.
Does he not leave the ninety-nine
in the open country and
go after the lost sheep
until he finds it?
Luke 15:3-4

13
Miracles

Today,
step into a day of miracles.

You breathe –
your lungs exchange gases.

You see – your eyes take in colors and
shapes and your brain interprets.

You hear – sound waves vibrate
tiny bones in your ears.

You feel – microscopic nerves in your
fingertips sense what you touch.

God created you to be amazing!
Today, remember what a
miracle you are.

So God created man
in his own image,
in the image of God
he created him;
male and female
he created them.
Genesis 1:27

Here dies another day
during which I have had
eyes, ears, hands
and the great world around me;
and tomorrow begins another.
Why am I allowed two?
G. K. Chesterton

14
Hearts

The shape of a heart says, "I love you."

Look around today.
Look for the shape of a heart.
It could surprise you.

In a cloud.
A shadow.
A leaf.
A puddle.

With each heart you see,
imagine God sending you a Valentine.
Be aware of His love today.

He is saying over and over:

"I love you."

May the Lord direct your hearts into
God's love and Christ's perseverance.
2 Thessalonians 3:5

It is love alone
that gives worth
to all things.
Teresa of Avila

15
Loving Looks

A woman accused of adultery is
brought before Jesus.
For a moment you are that woman.

What have you done that people
would condemn you? What mistakes
have you made along the way?

The woman faced an angry crowd.
Who is angry with you?
Who feels that you should be
punished?

Jesus looks at her with love.
Hear His words for her:
"I do not condemn you.
Go and sin no more."
His words are for you too.

Therefore, there is now no condemnation
for those who are in Christ Jesus.
Romans 8:1

Always have compassion,
for all of us have sinned.
Saint Francis of Assisi

16
A Shower of Love

You are standing in the rain
holding an umbrella over your head.
Listen to the drops hitting the fabric.
See the drips coming off of the surface.
Imagine the rain is God's love
showering down all around you.
The umbrella protects you – but
it keeps you from the refreshment
of the cool water.

Name the obstacles that keep
you from receiving God's love.
Unworthiness? Anger? Fear? Unbelief?

Can you release them?
In your mind tip the umbrella down and
let the rain wash over you.
Feel God's love.

And I am convinced
that neither death nor life,
neither angels nor demons,
neither the present nor the future,
nor any powers,
neither height nor depth,
nor anything else in all creation,
will be able to separate us
from the love of God
that is in Christ Jesus our Lord.
Romans 8:38-39

We should be astonished at the
goodness of God, stunned that He
should bother to call us by name, our
mouths wide open at His love,
bewildered that at this very moment we
are standing on holy ground.
Brennan Manning

17
God's Gifts

God has gifts for you today.
Consider these words of Saint Patrick:

I arise today, through
God's strength to pilot me;
God's might to uphold me,
God's wisdom to guide me,
God's ear to hear me,
God's word to speak for me,
God's hand to guard me,
God's way to lie before me,
God's shield to protect me.

What do you need from God today?
Strength? Wisdom?
Guidance? Protection?
Accept these love gifts from
the One who loves you.

And now these three remain:
faith, hope and love.
But the greatest of these is love.
1 Corinthians 13:13

Your soul is called
to raise itself to God
by the elevator of love
and not to climb
the rough stairway of fear.
Saint Therese of Lisieux

18
Body Prayer

Take time to appreciate your body.
You are wonderfully made!

Sit in a comfortable position.
Touch your head and say:
I am wonderfully made.
Then your eyes:
I am wonderfully made.
Your mouth:
I am wonderfully made.
Your ears:
I am wonderfully made.
Move down your body appreciating each
part right to your toes.

Then rest.
God made you.
Your body is perfect and wonderful.

I praise you because I am
fearfully and wonderfully made;
your works are wonderful,
I know that full well.
Psalm 139:14

What God made,
God loves, because
it's inconceivable
that God should
make anything that
He didn't love.
A. W. Tozer

19
Come!

You are traveling with a crowd of people.
There is excitement around you
as you all press forward.
You have dressed in your best:
embroidered robes and silks.
Fragrant perfumes.
You are going to see the King.

You move with the crowd.
Feel the excitement.
The anticipation.
You hurry forward down the
palace halls, through huge portals.
Then…the throne room.
The door opens and you enter the
presence of the King!
He reaches out in love for you.
Embrace your King!

Listen, O daughter,
consider and give ear:
Forget your people
and your father's house.
The king is enthralled by your beauty;
honor him for he is your lord.
Psalm 45:10-11

On the darkest days,
when I feel inadequate,
unloved and unworthy,
I remember whose daughter I am
and I straighten my crown.
Anonymous

20
Be Loved

Breathe in.
Feel the air go into your lungs.
Breathe out.
Feel the air go out.

Now, breathe in love.
Think of the words, "Be loved."
As the air fills your lungs
let God's love fill you.
Breathe out the word, "Love."
Let your love breathe out into the world.

Be loved.
Love.
Be loved.
Love.

Breathe love often today.

Self-love whispers in one ear
and the love of God in the other.
The first is restless, bold, eager,
and impetuous; the other is simple
peaceful, and speaks but a
few words in a mild and gentle voice.
Fenelon

He has taken me to the banquet hall,
and his banner over me is love.
Song of Songs 2:4

21
Dog Days

Share a smile with God.
Think of all the kinds of dogs.
What was God thinking
as He made them?

Tiny Pekingese.
Long-bodied Dachshund.
Curly puff of Poodle.
Flat-nosed Pug.
Giant Great Dane.
Shaggy Sheep Dog.
The endless variety
of mixed breeds.

People are the only living things that can
share a smile with God.
Enjoy His dogs today.
Think of how He loves to delight you!

Delight yourself in the Lord
and he will give you the
desires of your heart.
Psalm 37:4

Dogs are the closest we come to
knowing the divine love of God on this
side of eternity. They love me all the
time, no matter what.
Anne Lamott

22
Love Others

Throughout the day
ask God to let you love others
with His love.

As you encounter people, love them.

Your barista.
The man on the bus.
A coworker.
A child on the playground.

Think loving thoughts:
God, love him.
God, show her Your love.
God, bless them.
God, protect him today.

As you pray for God's love for others,
you will find it for yourself as well.

If instead of a gem,
or even a flower,
we should cast the gift
of a loving thought
into the heart of a friend,
that would be giving
as the angels give.
George MacDonald

Dear friends,
let us love one another,
for love comes from God.
Everyone who loves
has been born of God
and knows God.
1 John 4:7

23
See Clearly

God loves you.
But can you see Him?

Think of a window covered with grime.
You want to see outside.
But it is hard to see through the dirt.
You want to see God.
Ask God to show Himself to you.
In your mind, wipe the dirty glass
and a small opening clears. Light!
You get a glimpse of a beautiful vista.
Give a squirt of cleaner and wipe again.
What do you see?
More light. More beauty.

In the same way seek to know God.
Keep going. Keep asking.
Slowly you will see Him more and more.

And so we know and rely
on the love God has for us.
God is love.
Whoever lives in love
lives in God,
and God in him.
1 John 4:16

Though our feelings come and go,
God's love for us does not.
C. S. Lewis

24
Time Travel

Let's go back in time.
Back before you were hurt by the world.
You are a small child – dearly loved by
God who created you.

Wrap your arms around yourself.
Love yourself as a small child. Tell your
child-self how wonderful you are.
Dear.
Precious.
Unique.
Loved by God.

Tell your adult-self those same words.
You are wonderful.
Dear. Precious. Unique.
You are loved by God.
It is true.

The Lord appeared to us
in the past, saying:
"I have loved you with an
everlasting love;
I have drawn you with
loving kindness."
Jeremiah 31:3

The spiritual life starts at the moment you
can go beyond all the wounds and claim
that there was a love that was
perfect and unlimited, long before
that perfect love became
reflected in the imperfect
and limited love of people.
The spiritual life starts where
you dare to claim the first love.
Henri Nouwen

25
Words of Love

God's love is not like our love.
God is patient.
God is kind.
He does not envy.
He does not boast.
He is not proud.
He is not easily angered.
He keeps no record of wrongs.
God does not delight in evil
but rejoices with the truth.
God always protects. Always trusts.
Always hopes. Always perseveres.
God's love never fails.

What do you need today from God?
Kindness? Protection? Trust?
Carry these words of love with you today.
God's love will not fail you.

Love is patient, love is kind.
It does not envy, it does not boast, it is
not proud. It is not rude, it is not self-
seeking, it is not easily angered,
it keeps no record of wrongs.
Love does not delight
in evil but rejoices with the truth.
It always protects, always trusts,
always hopes, always perseveres.
Love never fails.
1 Corinthians 13:4-8

The first act of love is always
the giving of attention.
Dallas Willard

26
Love Table

Sit at a table or imagine a table.
Look around at the empty chairs.
Now, fill them with people you love
and ones who have loved you.
You decide who comes.

Grandmother.
Teacher.
Friend.
Neighbor.
Parent.

Look back across the years
and fill your table with love.
Imagine each one present for you.
Thank God for each person at your table.
He made them. He gave them to you.
He loves you that much.

At times our own light goes out and is
rekindled by a spark from another
person. Each of us has cause to think
with deep gratitude of those who have
lighted the flame within us.
Albert Schweitzer

For you are a chosen people,
a royal priesthood, a holy nation,
a people belonging to God,
that you may declare the praises of him
who called you out of darkness
into his wonderful light.
1 Peter 2:9

27
Shades of Green

Look out at the trees and plants.
How many shades of green do you see?
Name as many as you can.

Jade Green.
Olive Green.
Forest Green.
Lime Green.
Kelly Green.

There are not enough names for the
subtle shades and hues of each leaf,
each blade of grass, each pine needle,
each green vine.
The world is a lavish palette of colors,
created by God.
Relish the gift of green today.
How He loves you.

Thus the heavens and the earth were
completed in all their vast array.
Genesis 2:1

God loves each of us
as if there were only one of us.
Saint Augustine

28
Safe Love

Your soul rests in a tender place
deep inside of you.
We all have been wounded
by the world in some way.

The soul hides afraid.
Walls of protection surround it,
built up in response to hurt.

Today, sit in God's presence.
Don't rush.
Feel His love for you.

Let your heart open in the safety of
His love. He will not hurt you.
Your soul is safe with Him.

Come out, soul, into His safe love.

Even to your old age and gray hairs
I am he, I am he who will sustain you.
I have made you and I will carry you;
I will sustain you and I will rescue you.
Isaiah 46:4

The soul thrives not through our
accomplishments, but through
simply being with God.
John Ortberg

29
Sweet Times

Think back over your life.
What were the sweet times?
Not the just the big moments.
Think smaller.

The starfish you found on the beach.
Bulbs pushing up in spring.
An unexpected rainbow after a hard day.
A hummingbird's visit.
A baby's tiny foot.

Before you knew God,
He knew you.
Before you loved Him,
He loved you.
Each small, sweet time was
His love call to you.
Remember the sweet times.

If God had a refrigerator,
your picture would be on it.
If he had a wallet,
your photo would be in it.
He sends you flowers every spring
and a sunrise every morning.
Whenever you want to talk,
he'll listen.
He can live anywhere in the universe,
and he chose your heart. . .
Face it, friend.
He's crazy about you.
Max Lucado

We love because he first loved us.
1 John 4:19

30
Jesus Waits

You are coming to a house
that you know well.
As you walk up the driveway,
light shines out from the windows.
Inside you are expected.
Feel the warmth of knowing you
are welcome and loved.
You know that the table is set.
Your seat is ready.
Love waits.
Jesus waits.
You reach the door.
All you need to do is to knock
and the door will open with beams of
light and warmth. Hugs and love.

Will you knock?
He is waiting for you.

Ask and it will be given to you;
seek and you will find;
knock and the door will be
opened to you.
For everyone who asks receives;
he who seeks finds;
and to him who knocks,
the door will be opened.
Matthew 7:7-8

There is a door to which
you have the key,
and you are the sole keeper.
There is a latch no hand
can lift save yours.
No ruler, nor warrior, writer,
thinker: but only you.
O heart, hurry now and welcome your
King to sit by the warmth of your fire.
Henri Nouwen

And I pray that you,
being rooted and established in love,
may have power, together with all
the saints, to grasp how wide and long
and high and deep is the love of Christ,
and to know this love that surpasses
knowledge – that you may be filled
to the measure of all the fullness of God.
Ephesians 3:17-19

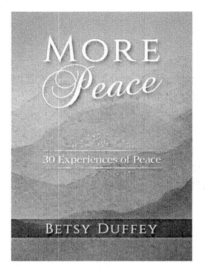

More Peace provides 30 short devotions
that bring peace.

Devotions focus on mindfulness, faith,
breath, and guided imagery to give a
handle of God's peace.

Sometimes we need to fight. With our own strength we can only go so far, but with God's strength we are powerful.

These 30 experiences are for those who want to fight in the strength of God.

Made in the USA
Columbia, SC
24 February 2022

56780648R00043